AF797628

1000 Confessions

Layered Voice Analysis for Investigators

Dale L. Tunnell, Ph.D.

Copyright

Copyright © 2022 Dale L. Tunnell, PhD

No portion of this book may be reproduced in any form without written permission from the publisher or author except as permitted by U.S. copyright law.

This publication provides accurate and authoritative information regarding the subject matter covered. It is sold with the understanding that neither the author nor the publisher is engaged in rendering legal, investment, accounting, or other professional services. While the publisher and author have used their best efforts in preparing this book, they make no representations or warranties concerning the accuracy or completeness of the book's content and expressly disclaim any implied warranties of merchantability or fitness for a particular purpose. No warranty may be created or extended by sales representatives or written sales materials. The advice and strategies contained herein may not be suitable for your situation. You should consult with a professional when appropriate. Neither the publisher nor the author shall be liable for any loss of profit or any other commercial damages, including but not limited to special, incidental, consequential, personal, or other damages.

Front cover image and book design by Dr. Dale Tunnell, Western Legends Research

PRINT ISBN: 978 1-7334212-6-3

eBOOK ISBN: 978 1-7334212- 7-0

FIRST EDITION

Contents

Reader Bonus Offer

Are you curious about what occurs behind the scenes? I've constructed a website with additional information and videos that might help you. As a bonus for reading this book, I want to offer you some tips and shortcuts that may help you advance your skills as an investigator and LVA operator. I continue to add new material, so I often return to review the latest and greatest.

I also put together a combination of eBooks, videos, and tools of interest. Head to my website and get free access to these little gems.

https://www.westernlegendsresearch.com/resources

Also, By Dale Tunnell, Ph.D.

Other Books Written by this Author

- Politics and Betrayal: Layered Voice Analysis (LVA) Defense for Newly Elected Leaders
- Resurrecting the Dead
- Decoding Treachery
- Codename: Language Inquisitor
- Computerized Psychiatric Content Analysis and Diagnosis in an Investigative Environment in Computer-

ized Content Analysis of Speech and Verbal Texts and its Many Applications

- Voice Frequency Analysis of Cognitive Stress Differences Between Men and Women During an Episodic Deception Task

Dedication

I dedicate this book to my wife, Deborah, who has always supported, nurtured, and guided me in pursuing the truth.

Acknowledgments

In every effort throughout life, a few supporting individuals have provided the knowledge and guidance necessary to reach one's goals. I want to express appreciation to those people.

First, I thank my military partner, former Marine Richard Lombardo. Despite the severe medical issues he experienced in the past year, he has continued his compassion and encouragement to my endeavors. He has been a steadfast friend and stalwart supporter throughout the time I have known him.

Next, I want to thank Amir Liberman, CEO of Nemesysco, Ltd. Without his help and support with training and access to software platforms, I would never have gained the knowledge and insight necessary to complete this book.

The same goes for Dr. Guy Van Damme, my European friend, and associate who has continuously provided me with alternative assessments and differing points of view.

There had to be a beginning to my training and journey searching for truth. I owe gratitude to the person who helped me begin my education: Avinoam Sapir, CEO of the Laboratory for Scientific Interrogation and SCAN – Scientific Content Analysis. His training was crucial in the furtherance of my education and development.

Also, thanks go to Dr. Robert Bechtel. He dedicated so much time and access to the works he and Dr. Louis Gottschalk and his continued support in the field of psychiatric content analysis.

And lastly, I owe a debt of gratitude to my former mentor and friend, Dr. Louis Gottschalk of the Gottschalk Institute, University of California, Irvine, for his relentless and sometimes painful guidance in my studies of content analysis. His invitation to participate as a contributor in his last book before he passed began my journey as an author. Thank you all for your support and friendship.

Who Should Read This Book?

I wrote this book to read in about an hour. I removed all the fluff and filler frequently added to texts to make them longer and look more impressive. Please read this book in one setting to gain insights as quickly and efficiently as possible. I do not want to waste anyone's time if this book isn't a good fit.

I would like you to read this entire section to see if *1000 Confessions: LVA for Investigators* is a wise investment worthy of your time and attention.

First, this book is not for the masses, but the concepts and practices are well-established and supported by years of research and psychological studies.

Accordingly, my focus is helping investigators add powerful analytical resources to solve cases and gain insight into the thinking processes of witnesses and suspects.

You can exponentially increase your investigative capabilities by utilizing the methods I describe in *1000 Confessions*. Quickly identify emotions and their impact on information concealment and intentional lies. Solve more cases by looking at anxiety, concentration, cognitive effort, confidence, and other factors uncovered using Layered Voice Analysis.

Specifically, I created this book for two types of people:

- The investigator who wants to excel in successful investigations and prosecutions and strives to develop a proven track record of credibility and a valued reputation.

- The intuitive investigator who wants his office to be successful and recognized for its superior credibility and unquestioned investigative abilities.

If you measure your success by accomplishment and skill, determination to excel, and a drive to successfully solve complex cases through legitimate investigative action, then I wrote *1000 Confessions* for you.

I spent nearly 42 years in law enforcement and over half that time in criminal investigations and intelligence. Working with some of the finest and most competent criminal justice and psychiatry mentors was a privilege. I gained tremendous insight into conscious and subconscious pattern recognition, content analysis, and psychiatric and psychological assessment.

I have worked with some of human nature's most skillful professionals and students. These specialists were and are giants in their profession.

Alternatively, I've met investigators who do not have a rudimentary understanding of the human mind nor the motivation to rise above a mediocre skill level that justifies their positions.

If you are one of those investigators whose only motivation is a paycheck or to climb the status ladder and mediocrity is what you ascribe to, don't waste time reading further. This book is not for you.

I wrote *1000 Confessions* with three reasons in mind:

- To fine-tune your skills and become a better-known and prominent specialist with superior critical skills to those of your colleagues.

- To give you information that investigators don't typically possess. The data will enable you to thoroughly understand witnesses and suspects of all stripes and position yourself as a powerful investigator.

- To educate you on the essential knowledge that will help you hone your abilities into an art form and become a true professional.

In today's law enforcement environment, many who decide to take up the badge and gun, whether local, state, or federal, look for a push-button solution to sorting good from the bad.

Push a button, and the suspect is lying. Push another button, and the witness tells the truth, conceals nothing of interest, and all details are enumerated.

The fact remains that no gadget or control can deliver clear-cut solutions.

However, you must search for those resources that help you reach ethical conclusions on your own. This book will provide a clear path for you to follow to apply independent and legitimate reasoning in finding solutions to the most demanding of investigative questions.

If you agree with these tenants, this book is for you, and you are already on your way to becoming highly recognized and sought-after for your skills.

- Establishing a good reputation, influence, and credibility takes work.

- Learning fundamentals in any endeavor is the foundation for building expertise.

- Becoming a professional in your investigative position should be an

> eventual goal of any person who wishes for superior skills to solve problems for others.

If you desire to move beyond your basic investigator training, add more skill, attain more credibility, broaden your experience, and reach a pinnacle of expertise you never thought possible, then I wrote *1000 Confessions* for you. **Keep reading!**

My Promise to You

I sincerely believe that the importance of becoming a successful investigator in a function that is so versatile yet incorporates so few experts is an endeavor worthy of anyone's goals.

I intend to provide you with advanced skills and support that will open your eyes and mind to becoming a "super" investigator. I want to motivate you to become superior in recognizing the power of patterns in speech and linguistic dynamics. You can elevate your skills to an art form rather than place a checkmark on a list of skills you need to impress others.

An investigator who correctly uses superior methodology with mindful dexterity can produce predictable and consistent results that far out-distances efforts and insight by peers.

Implementing the processes outlined in this book will propel your credibility and reputation as a recognized authority in investigations while gaining a superior insight into the cognitive functions and motivations of both witnesses and suspects.

You will also gain a higher quality of experience to enhance your exposure and reach levels of expertise you may not have thought possible.

That is my promise to you.

Introduction

As I progressed through my 40+ years of law enforcement, I searched for methods or a combination of techniques I could use to solve investigations successfully, regardless of complexity.

About halfway through my career, I became an investigator. I followed the route of most new investigators by attending every training module available. I learned a lot, and after five years, I became a regular investigator with at least moderate skills on par with my peers.

I searched for techniques I could apply to solve crimes and contribute to gaining confessions.

A confession was the measure of a successful investigation backed up by contributive evidence. Like many investigators, I viewed the confession as a single, culminating element leading to the case conclusion. I was wrong.

I overlooked that there may be multiple confessions in a single statement, not just about the incident under investigation. Numerous admissions resulting from patterns in linguistics, emotions, and cognitive processes were awaiting discovery but were hiding in a single conversation.

Eventually, I discovered that a successful case conclusion isn't about a single confession but a thousand *confessions* buried deep in human nature. Sometimes independent, sometimes not. Confessions are simply part of a larger whole. The final pattern tells the rest of the story.

Over several years, I discovered that I needed to solve many cases successfully to become a genuinely bona fide investigator who could speak with authority and recognized credibility. I needed to perfect skills not usually developed by most investigators.

I focused on gaining more skills as an interviewer and interrogator. I attended training by John E. Reid and Associates, Wicklander-Zulawski and Associates, and any activity I could find involving interviewing. My success developed gradually, but I was not nearly as good as I thought. Something was missing, and it was so essential I almost missed it. Simple to recognize, difficult to master.

What I almost missed was the relevance of language patterns in statements, both verbal and written. People speak in their language from patterns developed at an early age. If I could learn to garner information from these patterns, I could tune in to what information people might be hiding within written statements or interviews.

I searched for established analysis methods, but I couldn't find any training to help me develop what I considered the ultimate investigation. Becoming a quality investigator was a multi-step process, building a foundation of training and experience and then focusing on acquiring skills superior to elemental analysis.

I saw examples of what I wanted to do in specialized fields such as Questioned Documents Examiners, Polygraphists, Crime Scene Specialists, etc. But I was looking for something different, not typically found in training catalogs at the time, but that could help me focus on interpersonal communications to find those hidden tidbits of information often concealed by guilty parties.

I learned of a man named Avinoam Sapir, who ran a training program called the Laboratory of Scientific Interrogation in Phoenix, AZ. He presented a 3-day training series using a method they developed called Scientific Content Analysis (SCAN). The course taught investigators to find concealed information in language. His program focused on written documents or statements from witnesses and subjects.

Eventually, I took the course and practiced this skill until I could teach it. Using SCAN as my foundation, I developed additional training to add to SCAN. I was moderately successful in establishing a national training regimen and learned while I trained others. I called the program Forensic Linguistic

Patterning. I incorporated the training provided by Sapir into a broader framework, including psychological assessment.

Over time, investigators and prosecutors moved away from taking statements in writing and progressed to recorded communications, both audio and video. An investigator could still use SCAN, but the recordings required transcribing. Both time-consuming and expensive, law enforcement agencies no longer considered transcription and SCAN as favored investigative tools. Big mistake! The technique is viable and highly useful when coupled with other methods.

Newer investigators reared in a push-button society eventually looked for a more straightforward method to be successful. I have heard it expressed that SCAN takes too much work, and they have too much to do in their investigation to take the time to apply SCAN techniques. Whoever said an investigation was easy? A dedicated investigator does whatever it takes to solve a case legally. Taking the easy way out usually ends in a dismal failure. Just my opinion!

All my rant aside, I also looked for a better combination of techniques that would help me become more successful. I was pursuing my doctorate in psychology at this point in my career when I met another trailblazer. Dr. Louis Gottschalk, Professor Emeritus at the University of California, Irvine, developed a content analysis method called The Gottschalk-Gleser Content Analysis Scales.

He eventually wrote a book titled The Measurement of Psychological States Through the Content Analysis of Verbal Behavior, one of about a hundred books and studies he wrote over the years. All are challenging to read if you aren't a psychology major, but they pack lots of information.

Dr. Gottschalk became my mentor and friend, and he encouraged me to complete my degree in psychology using much of his methodology in Content Analysis. Now I had a highly significant and well-validated method to merge with those I had already discovered to increase my content analysis expertise.

Dissertation written. Committee satisfied. University approval granted. Degree completed! I was still missing something. Then I found a small Israeli company, Nemesysco, Ltd., located in Tel Aviv, Israel, that offered training in a new technology called Layered Voice Analysis (LVA). In 2007, I traveled to Tel Aviv to attend training in this unique technology. (More about LVA in a later chapter.)

The company's CEO, Amir Liberman, helped me develop my expertise in what I consider to be the most unique and comprehensive methods to identify linguistic and statistical patterns of language, emotion, and cognition. Coupled with my advanced degree in psychology, my previous training, and a career in law enforcement, I advanced my authority and credibility as a superior investigator. Ultimately, I became a Master Practitioner in Layered Voice Analysis (LVA).

Pay Close Attention

I hope you'll use the mechanisms I describe to solve more cases in less time than ever. An investigation with ample physical and circumstantial evidence may be enough for prosecution. But many cases lack material evidence. Ask yourself why so many investigators give up on those cases. They run into roadblocks because they only have their fallible intuition to fall back on. However, they can now gather direct leads from their suspect's language, emotions, and cognitive functions.

After working so long in criminal justice, I switched gears and began focusing on the political environment. Politics had become a cesspool of liars, self-aggrandizing narcissists, and inferior leaders. I felt it necessary to help those who wanted to do the right thing.

My journey didn't happen overnight. It required a continued regimen of training and development over 20 years to reach my goal.

Ultimately, I attained the position of Level III Authorized Trainer of LVA, one of only three Master Practitioners in the world. The other two are Dr. Guy Van Damme, Nemesysco Service Center, Africa, and Prof.

Alexey Gusev, Moscow State University, Russia.

I now use Layered Voice Analysis in a manner that helps me identify political corruption and write about it. Along with two other master practitioners in Europe and South Africa, I also train investigators to become skillful LVA operators using the investigative tools developed by Nemesysco, Ltd.

Continue reading to learn how to uncover information a witness or suspect doesn't want you to know and understand the secrets of hidden emotions in "The Deceptive Circuit."

But if this process doesn't appeal to you—there is no sense in wasting any more of your time. Stop here and give the book to someone else!

Why Do You Need an Investigative Tool?

A Bigger Gun; More Bullets!

A look at the history of criminal investigation shows that the field has changed dramatically since its inception. The first investigators had no training to investigate crimes; they often had only military experience. These men were often called "special agents" or "investigators."

Their duties included tracking down criminals, apprehending fugitives, and capturing spies. As crime became more prevalent, the need for skilled investigators grew. Investigators began to specialize in specific areas such as burglary, robbery, murder, and arson. Some investigators worked exclusively on one case, while others investigated multiple types.

As technology advanced, so did the tools available to investigators. Today forensic science plays a significant role in solving crimes. For example, fingerprints, hair samples, blood stains, and other evidence collected from crime scenes can provide crucial clues that lead to an arrest.

In addition to using scientific methods, modern investigators look for new tools and techniques to advance their capabilities. If you want to become a great investigator and solve more investigations in less time, advance beyond those traits that make you suitable. Accelerate your skills in the field of Layered Voice Analysis (LVA).

LVA is a fascinating technology originating from a division of science only minimally explored. I'll cover it more in other chapters but for now, suffice it to say there is room to excel in this field of endeavor. Once you become an LVA practitioner, you have already advanced beyond your peers' capacities.

This application relies on voice frequencies and time measurement to identify patterns of linguistics, emotion, and cognitive processes. These clues take the investigator into the seat of concealment and deception. But now, you are participating in psychology, neuropsychology, physiology, psycholinguistics, and psychiatry.

What is Layered Voice Analysis (LVA)?

A Golden Key

Each time you communicate with a person, you analyze what and how they say it. Volume, tone, clarity, etc., are signals we pick up. The voice signals anger, fear, excitement, uncertainty, possible health problems, and drug or alcohol consumption. Almost everyone performs voice analysis daily, recognizing how others feel and their emotions. LVA focuses on indications derived from voice frequencies and time domains to assess emotions, mental state, and level of honesty.

When we communicate with others, we often voluntarily change our tone of speech to reflect a particular mood, such as happy, firm, uncertain, or angry. We're always revealing our true feelings through our words and actions. But we frequently control our voices to mask our true feelings. Camouflaging our feelings helps avoid vulnerability.

Traditionally, the phonetic analysis focuses on the sounds one hears during conversations. However, LVA goes beyond the audible range and listens deeper into the voice, identifying the traces of its uncontrolled qualities.

These qualities include the genuine reactions people feel while expressing their thoughts. Neural networks tie ideas to the voice, and by monitoring the voice's deep parameters, we can identify thinking processes and feelings.

Nemesysco invented new measurement algorithms for capturing and computing these feelings. They're the basis of the emotion detection technology in the LVA. Together with a set of baseline measures, these algorithms function in every emotion analysis process LVA performs!

While most of the LVAs' parameters are novel, sometimes the expressed and enduring values inside them may carry emotional analytic weight too. For the sake of this discussion, we'll include any vocal element that has dynamic content as relevant.

Nemesysco's approach to layered voice analysis involves using multiple fields of science, including phonetics, psychology, psychophysiology, and neuroscience.

Terms of Relevance

Here Are Some Terms Related to the LVA That You Should Become Familiar With:

Sensations are genuine feelings we feel without needing any logical activity. They include in the LVA technology the fundamental three trends: stress, excitement, and confusion. Other versions of LVA technology also calculate emotional energy as the fourth sensation.

Emotions are the more profound expressions of emotional reactions and are often used to describe the result of the perception of a situation. They include hesitation, concentration, anticipation, arousal, excitement, cognitive elevation, intense thinking, embarrassment, and imagination.

Expressions are the classical emotions: happy, sad, and angry.

Stress is your body's response to a perceived threat. The amygdala part of your brain identifies a potential danger and sends an alarm to your body to prepare for action; the ancient brain assumes control and transitions your body into "survival mode." At this point, your only desire is not to be where the danger is. Any alternative is acceptable.

Excitement is the opposite of stress. When you're excited, you feel happy and energetic. You may even get anxious because you want to start doing something immediately.

Cognitive stress or cognitive dissonance is a conflict between two or more different thoughts or beliefs.

You may be familiar with 20th-century emotional theories. However, these theories are less relevant when classifying emotions using LVA.

Nemesysco deliberately left out different classifications when creating the LVA. They intended to stick to the facts collected from daily routines and not get caught up in classifying things into neat categories.

Collecting genuine field findings was crucial to learning about LVA, its unique capabilities, and its limits. I should mention one essential limit and place it into context. Voice analysis, by its nature, is a susceptible operation.

The level of input and background noise easily influence the LVA. The quality of equipment, compression techniques, and external stimuli the tested subjects experience as they speak impact LVA determinations. All these factors can significantly impact how much data we get from the voice recording.

However, despite those limitations, LVA can still extract helpful information from almost every voice signal. But common sense and careful consideration must be applied in every step of the analysis process.

What is the Deceptive Circuit?

Typically, when we experience a sensation, it is positive (Excitement), negative (Stress), or we do not know yet (Confusion, Cognitive Stress).

Most often, a sensation will go in only one direction. Lies are the exception. Deceptive Circuits occur in the instant moment when a person makes the decision, attempting to deviate from the sensation's natural path. Realizing that an outcome will not be favorable, a person tries to change the future by concealing information or lying. This realization is a highly significant event. "Changing your future" is exciting, confusing, and stressful simultaneously with varying intensities of emotion.

LVA is an exceptionally sophisticated technology that measures psychological states through algorithmic analysis and presents the outcome in a statistical format. I've stated that the LVA measures approximately 150 parameters of the human voice. That is a conservative number. It presents an operational level with which we can currently work. As more research occurs, practitioners identify more parameters and meanings, adding to undiscovered complexities and dynamics that are superior to those we now recognize.

I can teach any investigator to use LVA technology. There is a significant number of operators throughout the world who currently use some derivative of the LVA. The system is not cheap and ranges in price from a few thousand dollars for a canned program to well over $50K for the more complex security and investigative tools. However, requesting assistance from a Level II operator can often provide details you wouldn't discover.

But remember that these operators, while having been well-trained, are not master practitioners, of which there are only three worldwide. And in the field of investigation with Layered Voice Analysis, you have a book written by a Master Practitioner and the only one in North America.

Contact me anytime to discuss the LVA and how it might apply to your future. We may discover solutions to questions you have yet to recognize.

Tell Me More About Layered Voice Analysis

Aren't You a Little Curious?

Understanding human emotions and motivations have been a critical challenge in every aspect of our lives, from career choices to personal relationships to scientific discoveries, from infancy to maturity, childhood to adulthood, and adolescence to old age. The better we understand human emotions and motivations, the more effectively we can react and interact.

Through continual development, the originator of the LVA, Nemesysco, Ltd., collaborates with experts from many relevant fields. These include psychology/criminology, phonetics/phonology, psychiatry, mathematics, and linguistics. The LVA focuses on the human voice's unpredictable yet phonetic properties to identify deceptive intentions in real-life situations.

The technology operates on a patented set of vocal parameters discovered through research correlated with specific human emotions and detected deceptive intentions combined. These vocal parameters were found by analyzing audio files from various languages and settings, such as police interrogations, call centers, controlled experiments, etc.

Many of the parameters employed by Nemesysco's LVA technology are novel in phonetics, focusing on the unpredictable yet speech-related properties of the human voice.

Nemesysco adapted Layered Voice Analysis for many professional applications, including formal police investigations, security clearance screening, recruiting, personality testing, quality control monitoring, intelligence gathering, lawful interception, and so on.

The "Emotional Diamond."

Nemesysco created the Emotional Diamond concept in 2012 to simplify and visualize the complex human emotional response detected by Layered Voice Analysis. The idea arose from the observation that people's emotional responses vary depending on the situation. Knowing what they think and feel is difficult unless you ask someone directly, assuming they answer honestly.

Many businesses use questionnaires to assess employees' attitudes toward a specific topic. However, such approaches frequently involve lengthy interviews that consume excessive time and energy. So, how can one learn about another person without directly asking them?

The answer lies in studying voice responses to open-ended questions. It is a natural type of communication that lets people express themselves through speech. While a single language is not universal, LVA is not language-dependent.

Instead, LVA can assess any spoken communication regardless of the language used. Therefore, recognition of emotional states is not limited.

As a result, Nemesysco created the Emotional Diamond within the LVA process to assist those seeking to understand the dynamic conditions of others. This tool predicates the assumption that each emotion has a distinct shape. We can tell whether the feeling displayed is positive or negative by observing the shape of the diamond. Furthermore, the diamond can reveal information about the intensity of each emotion.

"Lie Detection" and LVA

Whether or not a lie is detected, it is still a lie. There are numerous types of lies, and each requires a different response. There is no single characteristic distinguishing a lie from the truth. We can only say that a lie is something that is purposefully false, whereas a true statement is something that is not knowingly false.

We classify lies into three types. A **lie of omission** occurs when you tell someone what they want to hear without providing any information. A **lie of commission** is another type of lie. These involve telling people false information. Finally, there is a third type of lie known as an **assertion lie**. These are purposefully false statements; they are not valid. We call these three types of lies omission, commission, and assertion because they all require some cognitive processing.

Of course, none of us are flawless. We all lie from time to time, especially when we are nervous. However, we usually catch ourselves lying and try to correct the error. While the question may appear simple, determining whether a given statement is true or false remains complicated.

It's one reason the LVA focuses on emotional patterns rather than lie detection. We analyze patterns to isolate cognitive effort and distortion. We already recognize the distinguishing characteristics of the designs and what they mean, but we need the LVA to make them visible.

What Are Some Ways to Use Layered Voice Analysis?

Limitless Possibilities!

Process of Layered Voice Analysis

Nemesysco's technology uses many novel parameters in phonetics, focusing on uncontrollable but phonetically unexplained human voice properties.

This technology adapts to meet the needs of professional users, from formal police investigations to security clearances, vetting and recruitment requirements to personality tests, call center quality monitoring to intelligence gathering, and lawful interception multi-channel analysis.

LVA technology, in its security applications, allows for a better understanding of your subject's mental state and emotional reaction at any given time by detecting hidden emotional cues in their speech.

The technology detects stress levels, cognitive processes, and emotional reactions reflected in subtle voice properties.

This information reveals how your subject thinks, what bothers him, what excites him, what parts of his speech he is unsure about, what questions need more attention, and what areas appear to be sensitive issues for the speaker.

LVA employs a novel mathematical process to detect various patterns and anomalies in speech flow and classify them in terms of stress, excitement, confusion, and other relevant emotional states discovered as highly correlated with these emotions through nearly twenty years of research.

The system recognizes and extracts relevant data from spoken language in real time. Each feature works independently, allowing us to process the same audio file using different techniques.

The LVA can be used in a polygraph question-and-answer format to generate graphs similar to those in a polygraph examination.

LVA can detect underlying emotions in a speaker regardless of language or speech tone. The system employs over 150 unregulated biological signals determining a speaker's emotional state.

In its commercial applications, the system allows an analyst to understand customer sentiments about goods and services even when they communicate using different accents and tones. Sub-phonic cues are excellent predictors of a speaker's emotional state. These inflections are inherent in the human voice and are unaffected by language, culture, gender, age, accent, or dialect.

Humans are aware of these signs, but because they are below our threshold recognition, they frequently ignore them. LVA technology accurately measures and analyzes these cues to reveal the speaker's genuine emotions. As a result, regardless of the interviewee's language proficiency or cultural background, LVA can provide accurate insights into the customer experience.

Endless Possibilities = Artificial Intelligence + Emotional Intelligence

Nemesysco introduced a new solution category called AI + EI: Artificial Intelligence algorithms and Emotional Intelligence. The company is the first to launch such a product. Its goal is to provide businesses with a powerful tool that combines the best of both worlds - the human element and the logic of artificial intelligence.

Aside from monitoring calls, analyzing conversations, and predicting customer behavior, the system can detect emotions and indicate the appropriate response. This technology enables businesses to make faster decisions and improve the quality of their customer interactions. They can use the system's insights to improve processes and increase productivity.

Examples of LVA Commercial Outcomes

LVA analyzes speech data captured via smartphone, softphone, VoIP, and other types. This analysis allows it to evaluate a speaker's emotional reaction as they speak. The LVA Score originates from these measurements. Based on their personality traits, the LVA Score indicates how likely a person is to behave in a certain way. LVA, for example, can help predict risks associated with new customers while reducing the risk of fraudulent claims in the insurance industry.

LVA improves contact center agent performance by monitoring their interactions with customers. LVA can identify critical conversations and escalate them to upper management.

Voice Analysis for Emotion Detection

LVA aids in accurately determining a person's mental state. Based on the emotional content of spoken words, LVA determines whether someone is angry, glad, sad, or neutral. LVA can assess the voice's ability to convey emotions.

LVA technology can assist organizations in increasing efficiency, reducing costs, and improving customer experience. Police worldwide are already using LVA technology to solve kidnappings, murders, and suicides. LVA is also used in hospitals to assess patients' health and in schools to track children's behavior.

A Digital Age Voice Analysis Platform for Recruitment and Human Resource Management

Voice analysis technology is gaining popularity in various industries, including human resources and recruitment. Indeed, human resources departments assess job candidates, evaluate performance, detect fraud, and forecast future behavior. But, in practice, how does voice analysis work? What do you need to be aware of about the technology itself?

Let's look at LVA-i, a pre-employment and personality testing platform that combines a proprietary voice analysis technology with carefully crafted questionnaires to provide a pleasant and unbiased evaluation experience. In addition, we'll go over the key features of the LVA-i human resources recruitment platform.

LVA-i is an application that allows businesses to conduct online assessments using advanced voice analysis technology. The software from Nemesysco analyzes recorded speech samples and produces detailed reports on the emotions expressed during the conversation. Employers can use the software to quickly assess the "integrity risk" potential of any job candidate or current employee in areas like honesty, loyalty, leadership ability, etc.

The system provides objective data that helps the employer and applicant/employee build trust and credibility. LVA-i is best suited for use in the recruitment industry, where it can help to create a fair and impartial selection process.

Nemesysco worked closely with recruiters worldwide to develop LVA-i into a comprehensive solution that provides everyone involved in the hiring process with the best understanding of each candidate's genuine character.

Layered Voice Analysis (LVA) is a sophisticated and non-invasive investigation and security technology used to assess emotions, personality, and risk. LVA platforms protect against fraud, aid in recruiting and serve as psychological diagnostic tools. Here is a list of Nemesysco applications and suggestions for where they might be most helpful. (You can find the descriptions on their website, Nemesysco.com.)

LVA-i

LVA-i is a pre-employment integrity and personality evaluation platform that combines Nemesysco's proprietary voice analysis technology with carefully crafted questionnaires to create a pleasant and unbiased evaluation environment with simple reports. The application can help detect internal fraud, prevent the theft of goods, equipment, and company funds, and promote fair hiring practices.

LVA-i detects critical personality traits and helps to prevent the leakage of sensitive information. It also helps organizations see potentially unwanted behaviors and inclinations to ensure that their employees are well-aligned with the organization's values, guidelines, and job requirements.

LVA-i deployed at the beginning of the recruitment process supports pre-employment vetting. This platform quickly identifies topics that could endanger organizations. As an organizational integrity tool, LVA-i conducts periodic assessments for all employees. And, when it comes to expanding an organization, LVA-i can help by administering personality tests to determine management skills, personality traits, and emotional stability - is this candidate the right fit for the job?

LVA-i provides testing in four ways:

- Interviewing procedure automated in a Person-PC interaction

- Structured phone/VoIP interview aided by an operator

- Making use of a third-party IVR or web service

- Incorporate the core LVA-i analytics into a system or website.

LVA-i is a user-friendly and intuitive platform. It does not discriminate based on age, gender, or ethnicity. It has automated report generation - intuitive and simple to use. It is language-independent and allows for rapid mass vetting.

InTone

Nemesysco's InTone application for call centers and the InTone Software Development Kit (SDK) help bring genuine emotion and risk detection to call centers - both as standalone applications and as integrable analytics engines.

It is critical to building rapport with customers and leads to customer satisfaction. InTone captures genuine emotional cues from customers and operators, provides real-time feedback to company representatives, and ensures they are and the InTone SDKehelpstomer's needs.

InTone assists customer service and sales teams. It is simple to install and configure the system to meet business needs. Operators and managers of various levels easily understand its user interfaces:

For Customers - Ensures that the company adequately addresses the customers' needs and identifies repeating customers' complaints while reducing call center workload.

Companies can detect and measure various emotions and mental states by incorporating the InTone SDK, such as stress, anger, embarrassment, satisfaction, excitement, rationality, and others. Every system designer can tailor the data display most relevant to their business processes and evaluation requirements.

The program significantly improves supervision capabilities by incorporating InTone SDK into a call center with unbiased and accurate real-time indicators. InTone analyzes recordings, and their output data can be leveraged in performance logs, agent progress reports, and customer insights.

The InTone SDK and Emotion Detection Platform detect and measure various emotions and cognitive states. Combined with an analytics engine, it also allows you to define, train, and see additional emotional conditions to meet specific customer needs.

InTone is the most sophisticated, flexible, and advanced voice analysis technology available, thanks to its unique combination of out-of-the-box detection of various emotions and the ability to train the system to detect other emotions of interest in real-time or from pre-recorded material.

InTone RA7 A.I.

The InTone RA7 A.I. risk assessment system, detects unique vocal characteristics in insurance claims indicating a high probability of fraud or information concealment. The software assesses the claimant's emotional reactions and provides consistent indications for relevant topics. InTone RA7 A .I. solutions are a combination of software components and carefully crafted conversation scripts covering each insurance case from every angle, measuring the claimant's emotional reactions and providing consistent indications for the relevant topics.

LVA 6.50

The LVA 6.50 is a professional investigation focus tool that employs Layered Voice Analysis technology. It can detect and measure various psychophysiological reactions indicative of changes in the tested party's perception, alerting the trained operator to follow its indications and leads.

The system will reveal the entire truth more quickly than ever before by getting to know your suspects much faster, using the combined professional knowledge skills and the high sensing capabilities of LVA. The LVA 6.50 has two modes of operation:

The investigator analyzes post-analysis of pre-recorded material at their discretion. LVA 6.50, unlike other systems, analyzes free and natural speech. It prefers to "listen to the thought process" because it provides the LVA with more voice data and helps to understand the suspect's or witness's thinking mood—things that a simple "yes or no" response cannot identify.

Because of this feature, it is also suitable for undercover work analysis. It analyzes free speech when investigating (where applicable by law) without the subject's knowledge or preparation. It is the most precise system of its type. It is not language dependent and does not require the subject's permission.

Is LVA 6.50 a suitable substitute for a polygraph? Possibly but not recommended. The polygraph has been used for over 100 years and is effective when used correctly. The products can work in tandem to uncover the truth.

LVA 6.50 complements (rather than competes) with the polygraph. Open conversations work better than yes/no questions.

When To Deploy Layered Voice Analysis Applications?

The Sooner, The Better!

I've learned the hard way to deploy LVA as soon as I have contact with a witness or suspect or a recording of their interview. As I was learning the capabilities of the LVA 6.50, I frequently failed to use it as an investigative tool.

Failing to use the platform immediately caused delays in my investigations, and I spent too much time re-tracing my steps. The LVA 6.50 is an investigations focus tool, which is what it accomplishes. The LVA 6.50 focuses your attention on details that afford you answers you might not otherwise discover.

You won't learn details on your own without lots of footwork and confusion. Many of the answers you seek surface immediately, sooner than you expect.

Please don't hesitate to contact me if you cannot deploy the LVA 6.50 because of limited funds or other barriers beyond your control. We can discuss your situation and find a solution or two to help you.

Please remember that our conversation is confidential and free. You don't need to worry about fees. Also, I don't have any financial affiliation with the developer of any of these platforms, and I am not obligated to share our contact without your permission.

So, could you call me? What will you lose? Other than a successful investigation.

What LVA Applications Should I Use?

The Most Effective for Your Needs, Of Course!

Most of the LVA programs have commercial and human resources applications. For an investigator or someone working in an intelligence-gathering capacity, even though LVA-i and InTone offer substantial versatility and valuable analytics, the specificity of the analysis is generally less robust than a platform designed specifically for criminal and security investigations.

While the LVA 6.50 currently has a premium price tag, it is the most reliable and comprehensive platform of all LVA products. Nemesysco developed it for security and criminal investigators, and it is, by far, the most thorough investigations focus tool available worldwide.

Nemesysco may have other thoughts. If you are considering a purchase, you should speak with a Nemesysco representative, who will help you with answers and suggestions to any questions you may have. And they're a fun group and highly informative.

If you plan on becoming a professional LVA operator or investigator, I recommend finding other programs to support your investigative conclusions. No technology is perfect and having a system of checks and balances only enhances your credibility. I'll discuss the methods I have in place in the remaining chapters. So, keep reading.

What Combination of Investigative Tools Do You Use?

I Go Right to the Smorgasbord!

The LVA presents you with a lot to consider. Training time and costs for the canned programs and those developed for commercial uses are inexpensive when one recognizes the time and financial losses associated with not using this system.

While I can use and sell several of these platforms, my primary application is the LVA 6.50 program, a comprehensive security and investigations tool disseminated only with the approval of Israel's Ministry of Defense. An investigator with a local, state, or federal government agency would probably receive support for dissemination.

It is highly sophisticated and not designed for use by a commercial enterprise. But, attained LVA 6.50 skills can be perishable over time. Lack of utilization can lead to diminished capabilities. Continuing to use it to perpetuate your skills would be a good idea.

To prevent the deterioration of my skills, I focus my efforts on applied research. In 2010, I conducted an LVA study of recorded telephone conversations of over 900 inmates and an excess of 15000 calls during six months. As far as I know, it is the only study of its type ever conducted. The results were exceptional because the agency intercepted substantial contraband and prevented assaults, suicides, and even homicides beyond the prison walls. Because the agency owned the data, we presented no formal study. However, anecdotally, the results were highly significant and should have led to more investigations and published results.

Today, I maintain my skill level by focusing on political figures who proffer communications that may be unreliable or beyond the boundaries of what I may consider rational thought. Media personalities are fascinating, and I often link repeated dogma to a central origin. Most of the time, the information derives from a political influence.

On occasion, the LVA presents an unbiased assessment beyond what I expected. I am amazed at what I discovered during a deep analysis of passionate responses. I frequently learn what the commentators conceal and discover fabrications and intentional deception.

But the political arena provides a target-rich environment, and who doesn't like to hear "the rest of the story?"

If I were to re-engage in criminal investigations or intelligence work, I would, without reservation, continue using the LVA 6.50 platform.

I also employ several other techniques to further any analysis. These include the following:

- Psychology
- Psycholinguistic Patterning
- Content Analysis
- Psychiatric Content Analysis and Diagnosis

In the following chapters, I'll provide more about the significance of each of these methods. However, using these methods is my form of checks and balances. This combination allows me to achieve the most profound and practical analysis possible.

Why Learn About Psychology?

If It Makes Your Job Easier, Then Why Not?

I learned long ago that understanding the human mind requires more than simply a beginner's skill level in the investigative arts. When explaining cognitive processing, or the brain's cognitive function, I tend to simplify the process more than most psychologists since I believe it is vital to present why specific patterning strategies work.

According to the KISS principle, the fewer moving parts, the better. It's not necessary to become a Ph.D. to reap the benefits of psychology, but having an intermediate comprehension of how a human thinks is crucial to any investigator.

The ability to research is one of the essential skills for investigators. You must know what, why, and how to obtain information. If you don't, you make decisions based on emotions rather than facts. And without good decision-making, you may limit yourself to wrong judgments. You certainly want to avoid bad judgments

Adequate Research is Essential. Here are Tips to Help You Do Just That

1. Start small. When you start researching something, take baby steps. Don't try to tackle everything at once. Instead, focus on one aspect of the topic. For example, to learn about a suspect, start by looking into past addresses. Once you've learned about those, move on to historical data such as criminal history, past investigations, family history, etc. Then look at job performance

and education. By starting small, you'll build up momentum.

2. Use online resources. Many free tools exist specifically to help you find relevant information. Some examples include Google Scholar, Factiva, and ProQuest Research Library. These sites allow you to search for academic articles, books, news stories, government documents, etc. They're great because they provide access to a wide range of sources.

3. Look beyond the headlines. News outlets often report on events in a sensational way. However, there's usually much more behind the scenes. You might even discover that the story you thought was true wasn't accurate. To avoid being misled, read the full article. Also, check the source. Did the author cite their sources? Was the information verified?

4. Ask questions. If you see exciting information, ask yourself whether it makes sense. Could the event happen? What evidence does the journalist or investigator offer to support the claim? How reliable is the source?

5. Think critically. Before you accept anything as fact, consider whether there's another explanation. Could the information be wrong? Or am I biased? Perhaps someone wants to sell you something. Maybe the person writing the article is trying to sell you on their schedule. If you question the presentation, stop reading and go back later.

Refining your critical thinking can help you make better decisions. You'll become a better problem solver and see things differently.

Psychology Can Help You Become More Empathetic to People Around You

Psychologists are experts at understanding human behavior. They study why people do things and how they make decisions. Understanding human behavior allows them to predict future events and explain past actions. I believe psychology is one of the most valuable disciplines because it helps us to understand ourselves and others.

Understanding people's motives and behaviors gives insights into what makes them tick. You might ask: Why did he say that? What does she mean? How did he react to my comment? And so on. These questions give clues about what motivates someone and how they behave.

People often act unpredictably or surprisingly, which can lead to misunderstanding. You might notice something unusual when figuring out why someone worked a certain way. For example, maybe they didn't seem very happy to see you. Or perhaps they seemed upset despite smiling. Maybe they even laughed inappropriately.

If you want to know what triggers them, ask them directly. Ask them what they're thinking and feeling. Listen intently and pay attention to body language. If you don't understand why someone behaved in a particular way, ask them again. Sometimes they'll tell you themselves. Other times, they'll reveal it unintentionally.

If you can't get a read on someone, record them in an open conversation (with their permission) or download their videos from

Youtube.com. Find an LVA practitioner and send them the digital recording. You may or may not be amazed at what they find, but their analysis will undoubtedly add to your understanding of their actions.

Why Do Patterns Matter?

They Provide the Foundation for Your Investigation!

Patterns exist in many endeavors. For example, a crime scene may have several identifiable indicators, such as the location of the body, blood spatter, etc. A forensic accountant looks for financial increases and dispersals to distinguish patterns of corruption. A physician looks for medical patterns that lead to a diagnosis. The list of pattern examiners goes on and on.

The same is true with human behavior. A psychologist looks for patterns in people's actions. For example, if someone has developed a particular behavioral practice, they will likely continue similarly. If you are looking to identify a corrupt politician, you need to find out their pattern. Study their behavior, history, and language.

Patterns can predict involvement in a crime. Specifically, voice patterns often provide significant clues about how a person thinks. I use Layered Voice Analysis (LVA) to look for emotional, linguistic, and cognitive patterns to determine participation, concealment, and malintent.

All people emit measurable traits through their voices. By using sophisticated applications like Layered Voice Analysis (LVA), one can identify hidden intent, mental imbalance, sensitive issues, deception, and many other characteristics involving thought processes, which may benefit you. These processes show up in measurable patterns. These patterns provide a comprehensive roadmap for the professional practitioner to follow.

Numerous venues teach investigative patterning. However, language patterning is not so typical. It is one of the least trained techniques. If you are looking for an accelerated level of expertise, this training is crucial and, in some instances, may be one of the most beneficial in identifying deception. I provide a basic process anyone can learn in a book I wrote, *Decoding Treachery*, available on Amazon.com. If you go further than this book, you will already have an excellent assessment technique that 95% of most populations still need to possess.

I use two tools to identify patterns in human behavior. The first and most sophisticated is Layered Voice Analysis (LVA). The second tool is called Content Analysis. In this process, we look for patterns in word and phrase usage. We determine the meanings of words from the person's lexicon and construct a diagram that provides us with information from unintended subconscious disclosures (USD).

I also utilize a computerized derivative of content analysis with a program developed by Dr. Gottschalk and his partner, Dr. Robert Bechtel. They call the program Psychiatric Content Analysis and Diagnosis (PCAD 3- discussed later). Successfully validated and reliable, I use it to validate findings from the LVA.

LVA involves looking at approximately 150 parameters within time and frequency domains in the human voice. The LVA correlates these measurements with thinking processes. While the analysis process is automated, it does require subjective and objective introspection. We use content analysis to look for patterns in the text that the LVA analysis identifies. While Content Analysis may be language-specific, LVA is not. One doesn't have to recognize the language to utilize the LVA productively.

LVA assesses emotions, cognition, hidden intent, energy, concentration, arousal, and many other parameters detected in the human voice through a highly sophisticated analytical platform and minute changes within the conscious level of cognitive processing.

It has significant predictive power in identifying criminal activity and emotional traces associated with intentionally concealed information.

Investigations are about discovering patterns, no matter what tools one uses.

What Is Psycholinguistic Patterning?

Combines Language, Psychology and Patterns!

In 2018, I wrote a basic description of this technique for my website, westernlegendsresearch.com. I included it here:

Mental disorders may not readily appear to an analyst without a tool to aid the reasoned analysis. However, a mental disturbance may significantly alter the reliability of the information provided. Remember that just because a person is psychologically disturbed does not mean that the data they provide is invalid.

Comprehensive analytical methods are required to examine the integrity of information and the impact of any psychological factors that may affect the validity. There are currently numerous well-known and widely used techniques for determining the credibility of information presented orally.

These methods represent some observations about linguistic and lexical structure and word usage. Although frequently subjective, basic linguistic tenants have been used to evaluate verbal and written interaction in social sciences and humanities studies since the early 1960s.

Linguistic methods use the same criteria. Both physiological and verbal responses result from intentional or unintentional thought induced by memory stimuli detected through physical observation or linguistic evaluation.

Linguistic analyses of the two types represent the larger contexts of information available for evaluation. These methods suggest linguistically determining the subjects' lexical definitions and word count;

they should also provide a foundation for a broader examination, including psychological diagnosis, which may trigger behavioral responses.

An examination of psychological behavior should provide more than a snapshot of the outcome of verbal communication in a much broader context. Are you still with me?

Psycholinguistic Patterning identifies pathology, anxiety, depression, hostility, health-sickness issues, and other psychiatric effects. Psychiatric and psychological introspection combined with linguistic evaluation provides a proper data analysis. We use psycholinguistic methods to conduct these analyses.

What are Psycholinguistic Methods, and Why Should They Be Used?

In 2005, I combined the Scientific Content Analysis (SCAN) technique with the Psychiatric Content Analysis and Diagnosis

(PCAD) procedure to provide a broad-spectrum analysis of written statements. This combined technique is known as psycholinguistic patterning.

The examination of linguistic patterns in verbal communications, both written and auditory, that produces accurate information in furtherance of any inquiry is known as psycholinguistic patterning. It is a non-intrusive way of obtaining information from communications.

It enables us to look for indicators of truth or deception, hidden admissions or omissions, emotions, and investigative guidance. This method also aids in the identification of mental processes and psychiatric disorders that may have an impact on analytical outcomes. In other words, is the person making the statement trustworthy and free of cognitive impairments that would jeopardize the integrity of their story?

Through language observation, analysts use language structure and predetermine indicators or markers to identify information from written documents and conversations. In addition, we identify psychiatric and psychological aspects or patterns that may influence the meaning of a comment, statement, or confession. These constitute the evaluation procedure.

Everyone uses their own linguistic and psychological codes in their speech and writing. Individual psychiatric, cognitive, and language development, or psycholinguistics, leads to this evaluation process.

We can obtain information and reach accurate conclusions about the impact of the person's cognition on the reliability of the information provided by deciphering these unique psycholinguistic codes.

Consider an ordinary conversation. During the discussion, both parties communicate using a common language. However, their speech only sometimes has a unified meaning. Nobody interacts with the same goal or intent.

The conversation progresses by utilizing linguistic traits acquired individually during adolescent to adult cognitive development. As a result, each language is distinct. While words may share common meanings in context, the language content and psychological style of individuals will always differ.

This process yields the distinct and personal linguistic code used to communicate thoughts and ideas. Different language content can lead to confusion and misunderstanding even when both people express the same beliefs or concepts.

What Are the Main Objectives of Psycholinguist Patterning?

This type of analysis has two primary objectives. The first step is to gather information, and the second is to assess the accuracy of that information. The investigation analyzes each word against the broader context and its relationship to terms instead of reading or hearing the discourse context.

The story's integral parts of words and their connections to others provide accurate information, not the story itself. As a result, we concentrate on the word content and usage rather than the storyline.

The strategy involves examining the conversation for linguistic and psychological cues and patterns. Studying and evaluating these patterns enables us to detect deception and gain access to information not openly disclosed in communication. Psycholinguistic methodology statistically and objectively evaluates psychological parameters and linguistic usage.

Although there is an inherent need to be sincere, conscious efforts to deceive often overshadow this need due to fear of punishment or greed. Our society accepts the constant barrage of inaccuracies from authors, the media, friends, foes, and criminals.

This reality is how it is now and how it has always been. Each individual is a victim; only the severity determines the extent of the harm. We tolerate small lies in everyday life because they have little impact on the victim. What about deceptions involving money, medical needs, or personal relationships?

When do we refuse to accept lies leading to crimes and deaths, terrorism, and war? Despite the cynicism, honor, integrity, and truth appear to be critical but waning concepts and imply that deception is becoming the norm.

Manifesting the Mental State

If we look for specific indicators, any person's statement consistently demonstrates their state of mind. Active verbs, not passive, non-committal terms, may be indicators. "I drove away from my house," for example, instead of "I would normally drive away from my house." Both situations provide information. The first statement is emphatic, while the second is passive and non-committal.

Psycholinguistic patterning investigates word usage, frequency, grammatical structure, placement, phraseology, specific meaning, and tense. One can answer many questions by determining the true definition of each word or phrase in conversation and comparing the content to normative constructs of reality.

Is there an admission, or has something critical to a decision gone missing? It is necessary to recognize when deception occurs and in what context. What are the psychological causes? Lying is a natural part of human communication, but does deception mean "telling a lie" or "omitting information" critical to the story's accuracy?

Linguistic observation examines a statement as a blueprint to examine its foundation, structure, and parts. This explanation implies that context is of little importance when analyzing the content of a message.

The account's various interpersonal relationships, the subjective meaning attributed to each word, the central locations where we use certain words or phrases, and the variations between the different words or phrases are all fascinating.

Thousands of law enforcement and intelligence agencies use psycholinguistic patterning variations to conduct criminal, administrative, and national security investigations.

Psycholinguistic patterning now adds a psychological component to these analytical techniques, backed up by cutting-edge psychiatric science.

Is a Psychiatric Disorder Present?

When we examine statements, we are not looking for a clinical diagnosis to establish the presence of a psychiatric disorder. We are not attempting to treat an individual; the reader is not, in most cases, a licensed practitioner. On the other hand, a professional may recognize the possibility of a psychological pattern in the statement.

This analysis assists the examiner in gathering additional information to determine the validity of a statement. In other words, was the person in control of their faculties when they communicated, or were they psychologically or cognitively impaired?

What is Content Analysis?

Helps You Read the Fine Print!

Analysis of Textual Information

Content analysis is a method used to analyze textual information such as books, articles, webpages, videos, etc. This process involves reading and interpreting the text, classifying it, and summarizing the findings. As you might imagine, different methods for analyzing text depend on the document type analyzed.

I use relational analysis after I apply the LVA to a voice recording. The LVA identifies verbal cues that have some bearing on the topic discussed and the individual speaking. The verbal cues might be unintentional subconscious disclosures (USD) or some other relationship to time and distance. I also transcribe conversations to visually inspect words and phrases in their meanings and their connections to others.

I also use semantic analysis, looking for meaningful connections between words and concepts. A concept is a symbol that gains meaning through its relationship to other characters. In a relational study, I explore how one thing relates to another. A relational analysis supports the idea that there are three main components of thought: relations, objects, and processes. Links connect things; objects are what one thinks about, and functions describe how one goes about thinking. I use graphs or networks to show how these elements relate in a relational analysis. This analysis helps me understand how people's minds work.

Professionals use relational analyses in psychology, linguistics, education, sociology, anthropology, history, marketing, advertising, and many other fields. You might want to analyze text messages, emails, social media posts, online articles, books, or anything else.

A relational analysis is a type of content analysis where researchers look for patterns within text. This process involves finding connections between different pieces of information, such as words, phrases, sentences, paragraphs, etc., and coding those relations into something meaningful. You should know what types of words occur together most frequently or what topics are written by specific authors. You could even try to understand why people use particular terms, like "the" versus "a."

Once again, I raise the importance of patterns. The goal of a relational analysis is to uncover patterns in the data. These patterns might provide insights into human behavior, document structure, or word usage. They can help us answer questions like: What does this document teach me about my audience? How should I communicate with this group? Why did someone post this comment?

Issues of Reliability & Validity

Content analysis is one of the most common methods to evaluate online media. This method examines what people say about topics in text and video formats. Referred to as qualitative research, it focuses on the meaning of words, phrases, and sentences rather than numbers or data points. Researchers use content analysis to understand how people communicate ideas and feelings. They look at the organization and structure of messages.

Content analysis helps us see patterns and trends in communication. For example, we might ask questions like: What does the author mean when they use specific terms? How do authors organize information into paragraphs? What changes the tone of the writing over time? We could explore whether there are differences in how men and women write about specific issues.

There are several types of content analysis studies. Concept mapping is one of the most popular, where researchers develop a study topic model. Another approach is discourse analysis, which examines the structure of language. Still, another is a rhetorical analysis, which looks at the organization of arguments. And finally, there is textual analysis, which examines the written word.

Advantages of Content Analysis

Content analysis is a generic term bandied about without really being understood. But it's pretty simple. I like to say that it's just text analysis done right. The goal of textual analysis is to find patterns within data. For example, I might be interested to know whether certain words appear together. Or maybe I want to know how often specific phrases relate to each other. The textual analysis uses Natural Language Processing (NLP). It provides a way to analyze large amounts of unstructured text.

How do I use Content Analysis?

I use content analysis similarly to other analysts. I look at transcribed documents and search for patterns. However, in discovering these patterns, I am usually already aware of their meanings by using known criteria I have developed over several years.

My assessment, while sometimes time-consuming, achieves a more comprehensive understanding of the emotional forces at play by operating with established standards. I condensed these criteria in my book, *Decoding Treachery*, available on Ama zon.com. The material is essential for people who want a quick method to sort fact from fiction.

I also employ a computerized application called Psychiatric Content Analysis and Diagnosis (PCAD3) to validate psychological findings that might appear in the LVA results.

For example, if the LVA determines the presence of cognitive decline, I might call upon PCAD3 to see if the same results appear. I used this combination in 2018 when I analyzed Vice President Joe Biden. Both applications presented evidence of cognitive decline, but most of his political supporters attempted to hide what was obvious even to the uninformed.

Does it matter whether we distinguish between dementia and senility for public purposes? Either way, there is cognitive impairment.

What is Psychiatric Content Analysis and Diagnosis?

A Secret Weapon of Psychiatry!

What Are You Feeling?

The Gottschalk-Gleser Content Analysis Method is adaptive to many different neuropsychiatric dimensions. Extensive empirical research has established the validity and reliability of scales measuring various emotional and psychobiological states.

Several accepted scales comprise PCAD32. These include:

Anxiety (containing subscales for death, mutilation, separation, guilt, and diffuse fear) and outward anger are among the scales. The Anxiety Scale is classified into six subtypes: death, mutilation, alienation, guilt, shame, and diffuse or non-specific anxiety. Mutilation anxiety is synonymous with "castration" anxiety.

The **Hostility Scales** measure three types of the hostility of a transient rather than sustained effect.

The **Cognitive and Intellectual Impairment Scale** gauges alterations in a person's cognitive and intellectual abilities and recognizes long-lasting and irreversible changes.

The **Hope Scale** measures the optimism that a favorable outcome is likely to occur.

The **Human Relations Scale** assesses an individual's interest in and capacity for constructive human relationships. We have not found content categories that can cover achievement strivings and accomplishments relevant to all possible fields of endeavor.

It may be necessary to specify the achievement goals of the subjects studied.

The **Narcissistic Scale** should be considered experimental: no norms exist, and research continues. The realization that diagnosticians and therapists use speech as a significant source of information spurred the development of an objective and trustworthy method of assessing the magnitude of many psychological dimensions from natural language.

The content analysis approach to measuring psychological dimensions includes the strengths of both the self-report and the observer rating scale approaches. The Gottschalk-Gleser content analysis approach has undergone a thorough development process.

The Gottschalk-Gleser content analysis method provides a means of making many kinds of measurements in psychology and neuropsychiatry. These measurements assess the emotional status of medically ill patients, but they also work well when examining suspects or witnesses. Once LVA identifies some cognitive or potential mental health issue, PCAD3 is well-postured to conduct a computerized analysis and follow-up.

What is Your Opinion About Using These Tools?

Better Than Memorex!

When you match the skill level of a Master Practitioner with LVA and add a secondary review with Content Analysis and PCAD3, analytical results can be mind-blowing. Nothing else available can match it short of some classified programs run by the National Security Administration or other intelligence agencies. Speaking from experience and not having access to other similar programs, if there are any, I believe the sophistication of emotive investigation within the LVA is beyond comparison.

Unfortunately, poor business practices and follow-on laboratory-style research studies cloaked the LVA's capabilities at its inception in the United States. However, the application's popularity in Europe, Africa, South America, and the Pacific Rim demonstrates that the U.S. lags far behind other nations such as India, Japan, South Africa, and Mexico.

This lop-sided utilization provides a dynamic opportunity for individuals within North America to capture a significant market share not realized thus far and establish the notoriety of being a professional LVA operator.

However, commercialization within the U.S. is increasing its capacity for emotion detection in call centers, fraud detection in insurance companies, and employee selection and retention in HR departments. Still, the opportunity to expand your reputation in North America is significant.

As a nation, we missed the boat on the security and investigative application LVA provides. Numerous law enforcement, intelligence, and private agencies currently use the LVA but not on the scale of other countries mentioned above. Turf battles with polygraph associations using their powerful lobby also hampered the LVA's growth in the U.S.

They missed a critical issue that LVA is a unique add-on to the polygraph due to its passive detection capabilities. A practitioner doesn't need to have a subject present for analysis. No wires, cables, attachments, or tubes need to be attached, not to mention the unwillingness of a person to show up for a polygraph examination.

I've used the LVA and the accompanying applications for over fifteen years. I have found no combination of techniques superior to the LVA and its derivative programs. Whether you are looking for business intelligence, investigative support, criminal investigation, or national security intelligence acquisition, you should consider asking for help from someone who has mastered the nuances and investigative capacity of the LVA. Even better, become a Master Practitioner yourself.

People frequently ask me for examples of how I have employed the LVA. As a criminal investigator, I effectively used this system to solve cases. As I explained earlier, a derivative program of the LVA was tested successfully in a prison setting and led to discoveries of criminal activity resulting in prosecutions and administrative sanctions. More recently, I focused on the activities of notable politicians and celebrities. I wrote about some of these personalities in my book, *Codename: Language Inquisitor*, available on Amazon.com.

I wrote the book as a tongue-in-cheek assessment of people like Prince Andrew, the Duke of York (no more extended royalty), Joe and Hunter Biden, Adam Schiff, Devin Nunes, Nancy Pelosi, Donald J. Trump, and others. I only touched the surface of what their analyses revealed. The book was a light-hearted presentation of the LVA's capabilities, but the sinister capacity of these personalities was front and center.

So, do you think I should recommend this program to investigators? I do but with a caveat. Don't go there if you are not serious about learning what your witnesses and suspects conceal. Because some people hide details from you that are so personal, you might wish to avoid knowing about them. Also, I do not recommend using the LVA or its supporting applications without appropriate training. You'll waste time and money, and your results will be far less than stellar.

If, on the other hand, you decide you need assistance, and you contact me, the effort only costs a phone call. An open discussion about your problem and possible solutions is free, maybe relieving your worries without expense. In some instances, my active assistance is pro-bono, but all initial conversations have no obligations attached.

The Next Step

Your Call to Action

Congratulations! You have made progress toward tremendous success within the field of investigations. I hope I've given you a new perspective on LVA Technology and that you are eager to collaborate with me.

Imagine how you will feel knowing you solved the most complex investigations and boosted your professional skills, reputation, and credibility. You will be able to tell whether or not the person you interview provides truthful answers or conceals pertinent facts that will solve your case. Understanding the thinking processes of witnesses and suspects gives you the confidence to pursue an investigation.

I wrote this book, as I previously indicated, for these reasons:

- To change your focus from being an average investigator to becoming a well-known and prominent specialist with superior critical skills than your colleagues.

- To give you information that investigators don't typically possess. The data will enable you to thoroughly understand witnesses and suspects of all stripes and position yourself as a powerful investigator.

- To educate you on the essential knowledge that will help you hone your abilities into an art form and become a true professional.

If you enjoyed what you read and feel like working closely with me, let me ask you to think about and answer these three questions:

1. If you knew you could advance your skills well beyond the levels attained by your peers, would you apply all

your efforts to develop expertise as an LVA operator?

2. Do you believe your principles, reputation, and credibility are worth advancing?

3. Do you value having a professional by your side to offer guidance, act as a buffer and help you sort out the intricacies of LVA investigations?

If your responses were yes, yes, and yes, you currently have some options.

- You can put this book away and ignore my advice; (I hope you don't go with this one.)

- You can use the knowledge I provided and go it by yourself, or,

- You can develop your reputation and expert skills in record time with an LVA expert trainer as your guide. You can only suspend investigations if you run into dead ends due to unreliable information.

I'd like you to set up a strategy session with me to review your circumstances and get help.

By selecting the third option, you have nothing to lose if you are serious about becoming a professional LVA operator and investigator. The power of prediction and confirmation exists inside this one call. Your objectives are particular to you.

The goal of the conversation is to help you look over your particular circumstances and get some more details. But we won't know about solutions until we have this crucial discussion.

This call is **not** a sales call.

The call is a two-way interview to ensure that we both think this is a good match and find solutions for your future development.

You can ask me questions, and I'll ask you some. From there, we proceed. Typically, this call lasts between 20 and 30 minutes, but we'll keep talking until you're sure you're ready to work with me or you're ready to hang up.

You aren't under any obligation to do anything.

Your morals, ethics, reputation, and trustworthiness are essential to you. I feel the same way about my skills. These calls are the perfect litmus tests to determine if we are a good fit. It's an opportunity to meet and decide whether cooperating makes sense.

So that you know – the onus is on you. It's your call to action.

Please make an appointment with me right now. There is absolutely no cost, commitment, risk, or obligation.

How to Set Up Our Phone Call

What you should do is:

1. Please send me an email about your interest to dtunnell@westernlegendsresearch.com.

2. I will contact you to plan a Zoom conference or phone conversation.

I'm eager to hear from you and, more importantly, to work with you to build your expertise and notoriety.

Thank you,

Dr. Dale Tunnell

PS. If you are interested in training or purchasing a particular LVA application, please visit Nemesysco.com. These folks are happy to help you and answer any questions you have about their technology or applications. (They will probably collaborate with me to set up future training.)

Author's Bio

DR. DALE TUNNELL was born in Powell, Wyoming, in 1951. He is a decorated Vietnam veteran, married, and now enjoying retirement in Wright, Wyoming.

Trained in Layered Voice Analysis, Psycholinguistics, and Psychiatric Content Analysis and Diagnosis, Dale is a retired law enforcement officer with over forty years of service with federal, state, and local agencies. He earned his Master of Arts Degree in Management from Webster University and his Doctor of Philosophy Degree in Psychology from Capella University.

Dale received Beginning, Advanced, and Stage II training in Scientific Content Analysis (SCAN) from Avinoam Sapir at the Laboratory for Scientific Interrogation (LSI) in

Phoenix, Arizona. For a brief period, he was an instructor for LSI.

Louis Gottschalk, MD, Ph.D., of the University of California at Irvine, from whom he acquired his expertise in measuring psychological states through content analysis of verbal behavior, mentored Dale while he worked on his doctorate. Dale later co-authored a book about computerized content analysis in law enforcement investigations with Dr. Gottschalk and Dr. Robert Bechtel.

Dale became a research associate at the University of Arizona, *Center for Information, Technology, and Research (CITeR)*. Joining the Center's collaborative research efforts with federal agencies and American academic institutions, he advanced Layered Voice Analysis studies and refined his practitioner skills.

After retiring from law enforcement, Halcyon Group International selected Dale as the Director of Forensic Intelligence and Research, a Department of Defense contractor.

He is the author of six books and an active member of the National Army Security

Agency Association, the American Psychological Association, and the Linguistic Society of America.

Reader's Bonus Offer

Are you curious about what occurs behind the scenes? I've constructed a website with additional information and videos that might help you. As a bonus for reading this book, I want to offer you some tips and shortcuts that may help you advance your skills as an investigator and LVA operator. I continue to add new material, so I often return to review the latest and greatest.

I also put together a combination of eBooks, videos, and tools of interest. Head to my website and get free access to these little gems.

https://www.westernlegendsresearch.com/resources

A Small Request

I appreciate you taking the time to read *1000 Confessions: LVA for Investigators*. If you take my advice, you will have a greater chance of solving more cases in less time while escalating your capacity as a successful and professional investigator.

But I need to ask you if you would do something for me. Could you please give this book an honest review on Amazon?

The BEST way for people to pick what books to buy is through reviews. I read through every review to find suggestions for improvement.

Email me at dtunnell@westernlegendsresearch.com if you have any questions or want to let me know what you think of *1000*

Confessions: Layered Voice Analysis for Investigators. I would appreciate hearing from you.

Made in the USA
Monee, IL
04 November 2026

67375751R00075